REPRODUCTIVE AND SEXUAL HEALTH EDUCATION FOR ADOLESCENTS
NEEDS ASSESSMENT

Reproductive and Sexual Health Education for Adolescents

Needs Assessment

Dr. (Mrs.) Rajani R. Shirur
Professor
Dept. of Adult & Continuing Education
University of Madras
Madras (Tamil Nadu)

Discovery Publishing House
New Delhi-110 002

First Published-2000
Reprinted 2006
ISBN 81-7141-535-0

Published by:
Discovery Publishing House
4831/24, Ansari Road, Prahlad Street,
Daryaganj, New Delhi-110 002 (*INDIA*)
Phone: 3279245
Fax: 91-11-3253475
E-mail: dph@indiatimes.com

Printed at:
Arora Offset Press
Laxmi Nagar, Delhi 110 092.

Preface

International Conference on Population and Development (ICPD) held in 1994 in Cairo for the first time underlined the need for promoting adolescent reproductive health and rights. For strengthening the above approach, it is necessary that articulate young persons and NGO networks are involved actively in advocacy, education and training programmes in adolescent reproductive health and gender sensitivity and promote efforts to initiate open discussions and counselling on adolescent sexuality. Adolescents and youths should be trained and also used as trainers and counsellors for their peer group.

As one of the prerequisites for educating all adolescents and gaining their full participation, continuing efforts are being made to institutionalize population education including education on adolescent sexuality in schools and colleges. This will indeed improve the provision of reproductive health information to adolescents and youth within a friendly and facilitative learning environment.

It is unfortunate that we in India have not adopted any policy specific to reproductive health of adolescents. No attempts have ever been made to provide reproductive health services to in-school, out of school and employed adolescents. More important problem relates to inadequate communication skills on the part of health educators and science teachers in schools in reproductive health and education. An even greater concern is with the inhibition and contra positive attitude resulting in poor understanding and appreciation of sex education. It is not only the students but more so the teachers and parents who require training in establishing rapport with the adolescents to gain their confidence and in providing guidance and counselling on human sexuality.

In the circumstances, a study measuring the adolescents awareness, knowledge, attitudes and preferences, on various issues related to adolescent sexuality and reproductive choice and reproductive health will immensely benefit in formulating learning content and designing teaching learning strategies for adolescent students in schools and colleges.

The financial assistance extended for the study by the UGC/UNFPA is greatfully acknowledged. I am thankful also for the cooperation and assistance obtained from Dr. N.V.R. Kapali, Asst. Director, Population Education Resource Centre (PERC) and Dr. N. Nagarajan, Sr. Project Officer, PERC, Greatful thanks are also due to the school and college teachers who participated in this study.

Rajani R. Shirur

Contents

Chapter 1

Reproductive and Sexual Health Education—An Introduction

In India, a developing country with alarming and disquieting population growth spread over vast territories, the policy of controlling population growth to meet the requirements of sustainable socio-economic development is strongly promoted. Indeed, we have made significant achievements in terms of reducing fertility. Yet the demographic momentum is far from satisfactory and the population continues to grow creating considerable concern to the entire nation and the world as a whole.

The total population of India has reached 953.7 million in 1995 accounting for over 16 per cent of the world population. The world population is 5716.4 million and it is estimated that it would reach 8,294.3 million in 2025. The enormous and rapidly increasing population is perceived as a great strain on India's natural resources and ecological environment and a formidable obstacle for economic development.

India has made consistent efforts towards development and modernisation through its Five Years Plans in which the periodic review and revision of population policy to reduce the rate of population growth has become an integral part of socio-economic development. The Eighth Five Year Plan focused primarily on the social determinants such as female literacy, age at marriage, creation of employment opportunities for women to help improve their status in society. These factors are considered as important as achieving a reduction in infant mortality, improving as achieving a reduction in infant mortality, improving health and nutrition of pre-school children and providing a comprehensive package of maternal health care services.

Though there have been considerable improvement in the status of women's health the world over, the general status of women does not appear to have changed much. Increasingly women are gaining greater access to education thereby delaying marriage and child births. As large groups of women are consciously struggling for gender equity and for recognition of their vital role in the society, there have been corresponding increasing the educational attainment and opportunities as well for women. The efforts in India to link literacy programmes to people's everybody concerns have implied a change in their attitudes and behaviour. Besides, the while emphasis on family planning and women's rights have opened new vistas. All these have had their share of effects on the use of contraception and adoption of smaller family norm, which in turn have contributed to better reproductive health. Yet, about 1.3 million women around the world still die every year of reproductive health-related and largely preventable diseases. Further, in developing countries, reproductive health related problems represent one-third of the total diseases among women of child bearing age.

Many biological, social and cultural factors influence women's health. The low status of women in societies, early marriage, early and frequent child bring and food taboos during pregnancy, are the associated health risks as established by various field studies.

Improving reproductive health is essential for improving general health and it is the basis for women's empowerment and is also one of the foundations of social and economic development. Good reproductive health is essential for the early stablization of world population. Several studies have established the fact that couples and individuals who can make the choice have, on the whole, smaller families than those who cannot.

The number of couples using family planning and the demand for various types of contraceptives have raised dramatically in recent years. At least 350 million couples worldwide, however, lack access to full range of family planning methods. Surveys indicate that an additional 120 million women would be using family planning if more accurate information and affordable services are readily available. This also points out that the extended families and the community are more supportive. This number, nevertheless, does not include the growing number of sexually active unmarried individuals. Almost half a million women die each year from preventable pregnancy related causes, and many times that number suffer illness or injury, often permanent.

The 1994 Cairo International Conference on Population and Development (ICPD) emphasised that improving reproductive health, including adoption of family planning practices, is essential to human welfare and development. The ability of parents to choose the number, the time and spacing of their children is considered essential component of reproductive health.

At the same time, the world wide high incidence of sexually transmitted diseases (STDs) and the alarming rate of HIV/AIDS among people, particularly being very high in India and more among women and young children, are posing threats to the entire health management system.

The ICPD programme of action defines reproductive health as a state of complete physical, mental and social well-being, not merely the absence of disease or infirmity, in all matters related to reproductive, systems, functions and disease. The ICPD approach to reproductive health is based on meeting the total health needs of people, particularly those of women and girls.

Adolescent's Needs and Choices

Today, more than half the world's people are below the age of 25. About a third are between the ages of 10 and 24; some 80 percent of these live in developing countries. This means that worldwide large numbers of young people are in need of education and training, job, health care and housing. At the same time, all these young people have needs related to their physical and emotional development, particularly as they become aware of their sexuality and in many cases, become sexually active.

In much of the world, girls still traditionally marry young and start bearing children at an early age. Even today 18 per cent of girls in Asia, 16 per cent in Africa and 8 per cent in Latin America are married by age 15. At the same time, improvements in nutrition and health care have reduced the age at which puberty occurs. Consequently many young people have a longer interval between the onset of puberty and marriage. Deteriorating economic conditions in many countries place young people at increased risk of abusive, exploitative and unsafe sexual encounters.

Information, Education and Communication

The relationship between education and demographic and social change is one of interdependence. There is a close but complex relationship between education, marriage age, fertility, mortality, morbidity and activity. The increase in the education of women and girls contributes to greater empowerment of women, to a postponement of the age of marriage and to a reduction in the size of families. When mothers are better educated, their children's survival rate tends to increase.

The lack of accurate information on reproductive health and conflicting messages in the mass media are increasingly posing problems and confusion for young people. Informing young people about sexuality and reproductive health is a delicate subject. It is often argued that giving them such information promotes early sexual activity and violates tradition and parental mandates. Therefore, systematic and scientific education for young people, creating awareness on major population themes and giving them knowledge on human sexuality are major tasks for all of us.

In this context, all our literacy efforts, the programmes of post-literacy and continuing education for the out-of school youth should be so directed that population education becomes an essential component. Although women's education should be promoted primarily on the grounds of human rights and social justice, it has come to be regarded as one of the most promising catalysts of fertility change.

Strengthening Population Education Efforts

Our national efforts on population education are being reinforced and strengthened with the assistance from the United Nations Fund for Population Activities (UNFPA) at all levels - at the school level, in the higher education system both through the formal and non-formal means, and also at the community level. Integrating population education in adult literacy programmes will be highly beneficial in promoting awareness and knowledge on several population issues like right age of marriage, spacing, family norm (size), quality of life for the family, and the impact of population growth on the family, community and the country, health care of mothers, infants and children, their nutritional status and so on.

Population Education for people in the community is most important because inspite of more than four decades of family planning programmes, the data shows that only 43 per cent of the people use family planning measures in some form or other. Therefore the issues of accessibility to and utility of family planning measures themselves have remained yet critical and integral functions of population education programmes.

Population Education Projects were introduced in the State Resource Centres in 1987 for the purpose of disseminating population education messages to the community at large. Population Education in schools, colleges and universities is an important programme for educating young people who can learn to control events related to reproduction and making decisions on when to marry, when to have the first child, how many children to have, spacing between births etc. In population education peers or peer educators are specially trained and it is evidenced that they are helpful in creating better awareness than through a formal transfer of knowledge.

It does not however declaim the need for formal means of population education for adolescents. Population education through formal means can start with age-appropriate curricula at the school level and proceed gradually to higher education level i.e. both at the under graduate and post graduate levels. Major aims of paradigm shift in population education include enabling young women to achieve desirable level of reproductive health, and developing positive and responsible sexual and reproductive behaviour among young men and women.

Chapter 2

Education in Reproductive and Sexual Health for Adolescents

More than half of world population is under 25 years of age and over 80 percent of the 1.5 million young people aged 10-24 years live in developing countries. These young people face serious health hazards in modern times. More adolescent girls, in particular, are likely to suffer sexual abuse, violence and rape from which they need protection. A large number of adolescent boys and girls in the age group of 16-24 years start sex much before marriage in urban areas and start sex early due to early marriage in rural areas. Virtually all these adolescents are in need of education, information, counselling and health services with regard to their reproductive health, sexuality and responsible parenthood.

Besides, most adolescents are unguarded and are susceptible to several risks like

- Sexually Transmitted Diseases (STDs) including infection with Human-Immuno deficiency Virus (HIV) resulting in AIDS.
- Risks of pregnancy often leading to unsafe abortions and its complications.
- Too early pregnancy and child-bearing and consequent illnesses.
- Sexual coercion, violence and abuse.

These can endanger not only their physical health but also create long term emotional, economic and social impairment and losses. It is essential that these adolescents are protected from unwanted sex, early child bearing, unwanted pregnancies, unsafe abortions, STDs and HIV / AIDS.

Status of Health Care Services

A review of health care system in our country and the type of services provided clearly reveal that there is gross neglect of adolescents. There is also profound disparities between services provide to different targets. Our major thrust has thus far remained on arresting population growth by reducing birth rate. Therefore the health services have always been targeted more specifically to pregnant women, the infants and children below 6 years and then the nursing women. In fact, the adolescent growing girls who are prospective mothers and the adolescent boys are glaringly neglected.

Health care services system established by private sector also caters to only socio-economically privileged group and is unable to make any serious and long term impact on the rural health delivery system or the adolescent health or the reproductive issues of concern.

However, there is perceptible desirable shifts in the attitudes and efforts of all - the policy makers, the planners and the health delivery personal-towards improving the management of public health programmes. Much of the efforts are currently being directed towards improving the management of population programmes through restructuring and upgrading the service delivery, evolving new systems of monitoring and decision-making and resources building. These are, however, done with a view to not only enhance the quality of mother and child care but ultimately lead to total family welfare.

Since the beginning of the International Conference on Population and Development (ICPD) at Cairo, 1994 and the Being Conference on Women and Development, 1995, elaborate discussions were made on population, development and gender related issues which brought forth world wide support and concern to address specifically the adolescent issues and needs. There is scant provision of information, education and counselling on the health needs of adolescents and young adults in our country with specific reference to sexuality, reproductive health and reproductive rights including contraceptive methods.

There is absence of any empirical information available on the health and sexuality needs, the type of problems they face, the risks they encounter as adolescents or young adults and their sexual behaviour. This is probably so because our tradition-bound society itself has deterred people from undertaking such studies.

ICPD's Emphasis on Adolescent Reproductive Health

The ICPD conference for the first time extended formal recognition and concern for adolescent reproductive and sexual health. The programme of Action (POA) of ICPD stated that the adolescent needs are distinct from adult needs in this regard. When the basic health services provided to adolescents in our country are virtually absent or negligent, the provision of reproductive and sexual health education and health services and related counselling services in effect remains neglected and illusory.

The POA emphasizes the following.

1. The parents and other persons responsible for adolescence should provide appropriate direction and guidance in sexual and reproductive matters.
2. The adolescents need comprehensive information and access to services regarding reproductive health, pregnancy, abortion, child care including STDs, HIV/AIDS.
3. Young males need to be taught to respect their female counter-parts, share responsibility with them in rasing and managing the family, child care etc.
4. Young girls, particularly the poor, face considerable pressure to sexual abuse, violence and prostitution. They should be provided with educational and economic opportunities to become self reliant.

With the changing social and cultural norms and practices in the society, the roles and responsibilities of girls and women are also being altered considerably, though at a relaxed pace. This is particularly true of age of marriage, premarital sexuality, family structure and claim over independence of adolescent boys and girls. The adolescent need to be encouraged to be more responsible in their sexual behaviour and have to be provided with information and counselling services protect them from health services to protect them from health risk, sexual exploitation, abuse and violence.

Significance of Population Education

In the above context, population education for the students of schools, colleges and universities and out of school youths gain significance. Population education will help adolescents to make appropriate decisions regarding reproductive behaviour and health for one self as well as to guide others in making decisions. To make rational decisions on wide range of areas relation to their marriage, conception, reproductive health, child birth, child care, maternal care, contraception, nutrition etc., information should be available freely and dissemniated widely. These have to be accompanied also by civic, social, cultural, economic and political rights. Informed reproductive decision making involves assuming responsibility for making rational choices. And capacity for making responsible and rational choices in turn, is acquired not merely by information and knowledge but by creation of opportunities, appropriates, appropriate conditions and contexts for making decisions.

Achieving reproductive health and making rational decisions regarding reproductive behaviour are not isolated events but are products of interaction between various extraneous and internal factors; factors like knowledge of reproductive physiology, personal health and nutrition, sexuality and contraception etc. are important considerations.

IPPF Chapter on Sexual and Reproductive Rights

Knowledge on human rights and reproductive rights are of no less significance. The International Planned Parenthood Federation (IPPF) approved a Chapter on Sexual and Reproductive Rights based on Human Rights instruments. These rights include :

The right to

1. Life, Liberty and Security of the person
2. Equality and Freedom from all forms of discrimination
3. Privacy and Freedom of though
4. Information and Education
5. Choose whether or not to carry and to form and plan a family and decide whether or when to have children

6. Health care and health protection and enjoy the benefits of scientific progress
7. Freedom from torture and ill-treatment.

Thus the rights of women and the girl child become integral, inherent and inseparable part of universal Human Rights. Any population education programme is incomplete if it does not include education on reproductive and sexual health and reproductive rights.

Reproductive Health Approach

Investing in reproductive health of the adolescent boys and girls is critical but profitable to achieving the quality of individual health, family well-being and improving their economic productivity. Based on the above goals, a comprehensive approach to adolescent reproductive health must be made which should include.

— education on human sexuality to all students in schools and colleges
— improving enrolment and retention of girls in schools, degenderization of work and destereo typing sex-role perceptions and performance.
— providing free health services and counselling through schools and colleges.
— Effective teacher training on the physical, psychological and emotional growth and needs.
— employment oriented, skill based education for girls in schools and colleges for enabling economic independence and promoting self-reliance.
— public education and counselling of parents for mobilizing support to adolescents education on human sexuality.

There is general agreement on the needs of adolescents to be better prepared on reproduction-related health areas for developing readiness for marriage and parenthood. However, there is considerable disagreement and controversy regarding eduction on human sexuality. The controversy and the fear of controversy have blocked sex education programmes in schools and colleges for long. Nevertheless, with the bold and scientific intervention of UNFPA and with the support of UNESCO, large number of Family Life Education and Population Education programmes have been successfully implemented in several countries including India. In 1995, the UNFPA was supporting national and regional school programmes in 79 countries worldwide.

However, population education programmes, by and large in India, have not made much significant impact for the main reason that a large number of adolescents between the ages 10 to 19 years yet remain outside the educational institutions and are therefore unreachable.

Moreover, upto 1990s, the concern rapid population growth, was confined with a narrow focus on the relationship among population growth the national and the individual. As a result, students learned mainly small family norm and spacing which were assumed to motivate them to limit the size of their own families later. Further, initial programmes of population education to students were primarily organized outside the curriculum and little attempts were made to institutionalize population education.

Education in human sexuality or sex education whatsoever nomenclature it carriers, has from the beginning faced strong oppositions from both the teachers and the parents, each having different fears and inhibitions. Teachers felt uncomfortable and knew little about what and how to teach various topics and issues on human sexuality and parents feared that sex education will encourage sexual activity among students. There is resistance from the teachers also because they will that curricula will get overloaded.

Adolescent Education

With regard to school programme on population education, UNESCO has provided guidelines and desired that it should be age-appropriate and culture - friendly. While listing the components of a comprehensive programme, it is recommended, that the socio-cultural milieu of each country should be considered important and the adolescent education is stated to cover.

1. the physical aspects relating to the anatomy and physiology of reproductive systems, physical emotional and psychological changes during puberty, conception pregnancy and birth.

2. Sexual behaviour including sexual feelings, teenage pregnancies etc.
3. Sex roles; and
4. Sexually transmitted diseases including HIV/AIDS.

Population education covering the above areas is being implemented in the school in 29 States and Union Territories in the country and the NCERT is actively involved. Population education concepts and issues have been integrated into several subject areas such as economics, geography, civics, science and the languages at the secondary level.

Population education programme was initially introduced in the higher education system as part of extension and co-curricular activities and currently serious experiments are under way in several universities to integrate into the curriculum of first degree programmes as well as offer special courses at the P.G. levels. The college youths are thus being prepared not only for use in personal lives but also to take up catalytic role for formation of favourable attitudes, values and desirable behaviours.

A review of various curricula in different Humanities and Social Sciences subjects like Andragogy, Education, Sociology, Home science, Geography, Psychology etc., at the U.G. and P. G. levels in the universities and colleges indicates that certain broad topics/areas related to population education are already included.

Again at various points of time between 1990 and 1997, population Education Resource Centres (PERCs) established in 17 universities in India, with the UGC-UNFPA assistance have attempted to review the existing syllabi and incorporate new areas in population education. These efforts also appear to be more of theoretical exercise based on assumed needs rather than actual assessment based. Professionals in population education working in PERCs and elsewhere, appears after informal deliberations with teachers, peergroup and educationists, to have recommended and/or agreed upon the following broad areas/topics for teaching at the U.G. and P.G. levels.

— consequences of population growth
— encouragement of sexual abstinence
— reproductive health and physiology-care of reproductive system

- — gender equality and equity-women empowerment; education and employment promotion; women; poverty and technology
- — different contraceptive methods-fertility management and family size
- — responsible sexual behaviour and related values - readiness for marriage and parenthood.
- — human health and nutrition - Hygiene, health, immunization - vaccinations - mother and child health.
- — health hazards - drinking, smoking, drug addiction, STD, HIV/AIDS.
- — health policies and programmes
- — human rights and reproductive rights
- — environment and sustainable development - quality of life concepts - population, resources, environment and sustainable development - interrelationships.

With further elaboration and extension of above topics/ themes in accordance with the age/gender and experience of the learners, it is possible to successfully integrate them into different subjects/disciplines both in the school and higher education curricula.

However, core messages and key concepts in population education have to be developed on the basis of identified needs and learning demands of adolescents in schools and colleges. A scientifically developed need based and demand driven population education programme for boys and girls in schools and colleges will certainly help them to develop their knowledge, skills and attitudes for critical thinking and responsible decision making and for achieving quality life both at the level of individual and the community.

No doubt in promoting reproductive health among women, and adolescents in particular, education in human sexuality, sexual abuse including rape, premarital sex adolescent pregnancy, safe abortion, infections and disorders in the reproductive process, etc. will be of great significance. The adolescence and young adults should be saved from all the probable future trauma and suffering arising from ignorance, inadequate protection or absence or non availability of information and services related to human sexuality and reproduction.

Integrating Reproductive and Sexual Health Education

There are, however, obvious advantages and disadvantages of integrating reproductive and sexual health components into the curriculum.. Integrating these areas into various subjects may arouse less controversy and opposition than separate courses but may dilute the content. It may also intervene with the teaching-learning load by either overgrowing in one or few subject areas or creating conflict over the problems of substitutions and dropping out of certain other curricular units. An obvious limitation of integration would be with regard to training a large number of teachers, methods of training them, preparation of teaching-learning materials for students and teachers.

There is another important element of reproductive and sexual health education for the student group for consideration. It has to be accompanied by.

1. **Special Health Services** including health check-up, treatment of injuries, diagnosis and treatment of simple ailments, further referral services for serious ailments etc.
2. **Counselling Services** which should ensure guidance and help in preventing premarital sex and unwanted pregnancies, use of condom, safe abortion and avoidance of health risks like drug abuse, drinking, smoking sexual abuse, violence including STD and HIV/AIDS.

The counselling approach which is more personal and individualistic with open access to adolescents boys and girls will provide them scientific, appropriate and specific information on sexuality and reproductive health based on individual needs and problems. Otherwise, there is risk of adolescents turning to their peer group and the mass media whose information is often wrong, incomplete or misleading.

Counselling services therefore has to gain priority in the reproductive and sexual health education programme. It is then a major task to select and train counsellors or peer educators who are not only interest and motivated but also have skills to gain trust and confidence from the adolescent boys and girls.

Institutionalized population education programme with a major thrust on reproductive and sexual health will succeed only when it is linked with appropriate, adequate and regular health services coupled with counselling services provided within the institution.

Reference

1. State of World Population, UNFPA 1997
2. Population Reports : Series J. No. 41-43, Johns Hopkins School of Public Health, USA.
3. Review and Appraisal of the World Population of Action, 1994 Report, United Nations.
4. Halida Hanum Akther, Fundamental in Improving Human Welfare, Integration, International Review of Population and Reproductive Health, No. 51, Spring 1997.
5. Anthony R. Measham and Richard A. Heaver, India's Family Welfare, Moving to a Reproductive and Child Health Approach, World Bank, Washington, D.C. (2 volumes).

Chapter 3

The Rationale for the Study

The International Conference on Population and Development held at cairo in 1994 for the first time recognized the need for educating the adolescents with regard to their reproductive and sexual health. It was acknowledged that the adolescents' needs are distinct from that of adults and efforts are required to educate them about how to project themselves from various health risks like

— sexual violence and coercion including rape, sexual abuse etc.
— early pregnancy and child bearing with high risk of illness and death of mother and infants
— unintended or unwanted pregnancy leading to unsafe abortion and consequent complications.
— STD, HIV/AIDS etc.

As a group, having survived infancy and early childhood diseases, adolescents and young adults have other wise the lowest mortality rates as compared to other age groups. However, most of these adolescents, are unguarded and are in jeopardy with regard to the above health risks. While the family welfare and family planning services have helped and are continuing to help older adults of 25 years and above or all married women, in meeting their reproductive and other health needs, young people are largely left out. The adolescents are the workers, leaders and parents of tomorrow. Fulfilling their needs for health education and health services are the major tasks that lie ahead of our nation. It is essential that these young people are caught and taught early so that they are protected from unwanted sex, early child bearing unwanted pregnancies, unsafe abortions, STDs and HIV/AIDS.

Unmet Health Needs

A review of health care system and types of services provided closely reveals profound disparities between different targets. We find that unmarried adolescents are grossly ignored by the Government and even other voluntary health sectors. The current system is more specifically targeted to infants, children below 6 years and pregnant and nursing women.

The gross dismissal of the younger age-group particularly adolescents boys and girls as a target of less or least concern is probably due to high concern and consequent over - attention paid to married women. The major thrust, therefore, during the past four decades has remained on arresting population growth and reducing fertility through intensive family planning activities. The national population politics and health have also reflected the same trend by limiting their concerns to evolving various types and strategies of health and welfare interventions aimed at protecting the health of women and children. With the result, the adolescent growing girls who are prospective mothers are totally ignored.

It is not surprising therefore, to find scanty information available on the health and sexuality needs of adolescents, their knowledge on human sexuality and reproductive health, the types of physical and emotional problems they face and the risks they encounter. Ehile reviewing and reporting the research and development efforts on population issues, the World Population Plan of Action, 1994 points out the needs of adolescents in order to develop suitable policies and programmes and appropriate technologies.

"Human sexuality and gender relations are closely interrelated and together affect the ability of men and women to achieve and maintain sexual health and manage their reproductive lives. Equal relationships between men and women in matters of sexual relations and reproduction including full respect for the physical integrity of the human body, require mutual respect and willingness to accept irresponsibility for the consequence of sexual behaviour. (para 7.34 POA of ICPD, 1994).

It was in 1978, the health planners from 134 member countries of the United Nations met at Alma Ata in the Soviet Union and drew up a Health Charter aiming at bringing basic health services within the reach of every community and the individual. It was here that the popular plan "Health for All by the year 2000" was conceived. Yet unfortunately, the adolescents boys and girls who are a critical and vital group have failed to draw attention until now. It is obviously because health care in our country conventionally implies the curative aspect and not preventive care. Therefore married and pregnant women who are prone to risks due to diseases, infections etc. are treated with concern. And health care provisions also always include setting up community health clinics, training health workers, setting up immunization programmes for infants, children and pregnant women, dealing with childhood diseases, setting up maternity services and family planning programmes. There was apathy observed on the part of Government and the public towards education. Therefore, adolescents have neither access to health care nor to education, information and counselling on human sexuality.

The question of organising outreach programmes for adolescents - education and health care services separately for adolescents - also pose threats. Adolescents will not be allowed by parents and will dare not attend health clinics meant for married women in rural areas for it will be considered as a social stigma. To organise separate health care services and education in reproductive health to adolescents is also economically unviable and socially unacceptable. Therefore the problem becomes more acute. To some extent this can be resolved by integrating population education in the formal system at the school and higher eduction levels.

Gender Inequality, a Major Factor in Population Processes

Female illiteracy, gender inequality coupled with poverty determine the sexual behaviour of men and women. In India, women are not considered as producers of economic value, nor their work is considered as of any significance. Women are always subjected to make dominating, right from birth, male child being preferred and gaining priority over female child. Women's reproductive function alone is considered as of value, if at all there is any. This has resulted in ignoring all stages of life other than that of pregnancy and motherhood in women's lives.

Gender discrimination and the resulting denial of basic rights for making decisions on reproductive functions are unequivocally accepted as 'natural' or 'normal' often leading to sexual violence. Women have no voice or right to determine the choice of husbands, when to marry and what child (children) to beget and so on. Husbands, other male family members, and in-laws make most such decisions.

Role of Population Education in Eliminating Gender Bias

In this context population education becomes an essential tool for removing gender discrimination from the young minds, both and girls at tender age, to outgrow the spirit of supremacy for the boys and devaluation of girls by means of self-imposed lower self-esteem, self denial and the attitude of dependency. Population education at the school and college level should basically help students.

1. Identify gender inequalities and discrimination that are practiced and accepted as normal in various spheres of life.
2. analyze gender issues in their own personal experience and see how unjust and morally unacceptable the current situation is
3. change their perception on the rigid stereotyping of sex roles.
4. build readiness to change their attitudes to participate in all social, economic non-economic and domestic including parental roles
5. agree to establish democratic relationship and accept sharing of power between sexes in order to empower women and liberate them from a state of powerlessness and dependency.

With a clear and changed perception and understanding of their roles and responsibilities, the boys and girls would be helped to understand and assume their parental responsibilities more effectively.

Education on Human Sexuality

A review of curricular experiences organised for adolescents in the schools and colleges reveal that there are no special educational programmes concerned with sex education and reproductive health education. Nor are there any special clinics or services provided to the adolescents and young adults. In a very small way, few extension and co-curricular activities are being organised which however involve insignificant number of school and college students in urban area. With the adolescents in the age group of 13 to 21 years soon becoming sexually matured and active, many of them are likely to face health risks. Even so, their accessibility to factual information on sexual activities and health care is also meager or negligible. Developing readiness among the adolescents and young adults to enter marital union in a healthy manner is, therefore, very important.

Defining Adolescence

Adolescence is a stage of development transition. It bridges between childhood and adulthood and is considered generally to being at about 12 to 13 and to end in the late teens or early twenties. The period of adolescence is characterised by the physical, intellectual, temperamental and emotional change in their attitudes and behaviour. The W.H.O. has defined adolescence as :

— Progression from appearance of secondary sex characteristics (Puberty) to sexual and reproductive maturity.
— development of adult mental processes and adult identity
— transition from total socio-economic dependence to relative independence.

Though the latter conditions may not characterize an adolescent in India. Many definitions include the age group 10 to 19 while the WHO defines it to cover upto the age of 24 years.

Characteristics of Adolescents

In India, adolescents is traditionally viewed as an age of learning and strengthening the moral, spiritual and intellectual bases. It is, therefore, a period considered for the adolescents to strictly abstain from sexual and reproductive activity. However, the changing socio-cultural and technological era witnesses changes in the conceptual, attitudinal and behavioural aspects of society thus creating a need for education on human sexuality for adolescents.

Adolescents are usually in a state of comparatively good health. They have greater physical vigour and are curious in nature. Lack of scientific information on sexuality and the physiological change in adolescents drive them to explore, experiment and experience in the area of sexual behaviour along with the peer group. As a result, they gather little and incorrect information about sex, they do not know where to go and what to expect. Many may be unable to pay for medical assistance in times of need. Often the conditions prohibit or limit provision of contraceptive services or even information to adolescents. Even when the adolescents have access to information and services relating to sexuality, many contextual factors might influence their behaviour. The extent of communication between adolescents and their parents and other elders, their attitudes to social and sexual roles and the taboo nature of their sexual activity all influence adolescent's sexual behaviour.

Problems and Need Based Education on Human Sexuality

When we review the problems of adolescents and young adults, we find a wide range of views being held by people as influenced by the society and their culture. In some cultures, some start sex much early due to early marriage or due to free society, some start sex before marriage; some even change their sexual partners before they marry. Besides pregnancy at an early age puts young women's health at risk through child bearing or unsafe abortion.

For that matter adolescents are not to be viewed as problems though they face diverse problems like sexual insecurity and the probable abuse, correction or violence and so on. They need sex education, reproductive health education and guidance and counselling services that respond to their needs, earn their trust and win the support of their parents and the community members. These programmes will develop readiness for marital life among adolescents and young unmarried adults and will encourage responsible behaviour.

This group needs education to abstain from sex or use of condoms to prevent the risks, of STDs, HIV/AIDS including pregnancy. On the contrary, their accessibility to factual information on sexual activities and health care is meager or negligible.

Conflicting Views on Teaching Human Sexuality to Adolescents

A perpetual and inconclusive debate goes on among the teachers, educational planners, policy makers and programme managers in population education whether adolescents should learn about sex and reproduction from the schools and colleges. There is strong opposition to sex education in schools both from the teachers and parents. Consequently these young people often receive from unauthentic and unscientific sources, misleading, incomplete or wrong messages on sex and sexuality. There is also hesitation on the part of both teachers and parents, even if they feel that sex eduction is important, as to how to teach various concepts and themes relating to sexuality, reproduction etc. They need guidance and support in terms of methods and materials for teaching human sexuality, reproduction etc.

When properly not intervened through population education programmes, the faulty and misleading beliefs, inappropriate attitude to sexuality and unsound and impractical values developed in adolescents might lead to difficulties in sexual adjustment and reproductive activity in adulthood. In a restraining society which do not encourage explicit communication on sex behaviour between any group between parents and children, between teachers and students, many may remain quite uninformed or misinformed about sex and this might lead to problems in premarital life and maladjustments in marital life later. Adolescents should, therefore, be provided with environment that is conducive for them to learn the state of art in sexuality and develop appropriate attitudes and beliefs and values towards sex behaviour.

Male Involvement and Education for Boys

Solution to population problems have always focused on reducing births through efforts to popularise family planning programmes through persuasions or even coercion at times. And the art of persuasions and coercion has always been married women. Unfortunately, whatever reproductive health programmes are administrated in India thus far have neither included men as target audience for IEC activities nor promoted their active participation in reproductive health or family planning programmes. It is an undesirable situation that male dominance in interpersonal and household relationships make them key decision-makers in reproductive health matters also.

Reaching boys, therefore, at a young age through schools and college based population education programmes is an important strategy not only to craft awareness among them but to develop health attitudes to perceiving their role and developing partnership relationships with their counterparts so that participatory decisions are taken on matters relating to reproductive activities jointly. Institutionalization of population education will indeed help all adolescents to build awareness, increase knowledge and promote contraceptive use and safe sex, eliminate gender bias and avoid violent and undersirable behaviour.

Goals of Population Education

The definition of population education has changed considerably over the years. It is generally agreed that population education is a process of helping people understand the nature, causes and consequences of population process as they affect and are affected by individuals, families, communities and nations. Individuals and family decisions at the micro-level make definite impact on the broader population issues at the macro-level, and together form the basis for establishing priorities not only in planning population education programmes but also for determining and selection of content for teaching. Though population education is often linked with demography, human ecology and family life education. It is not synonymous with them. Rather it draws its content from a knowledge base from all these fields and others too, with variations according to the needs of the targets and situational demands.

The Need for the Present Study

The goals of population education for adolescents is not merely for reducing fertility or preventing adolescents pregnancies, STDs, HIV/AIDS etc. as it is commonly comprehended. Population education has broader goals to achieve beyond educating the small family norm, responsible parenthood and so on. In practice, the goals and content of population education should reflect the diversity of needs and behavioural patterns of school and college students. A basic goal of population education must be to convince students that they can control many of the future events in their lives including those relating to family life, sexuality and reproduction. However in formulating teaching - learning content for students in schools and colleges, we need to gather baseline information regarding their initial knowledge attitudes and beliefs with regard to sexuality and reproductive behaviour, health, gender issues, education etc. This would enable us to reconceptualise population education, establish clear objectives and formulate effective teaching learning strategies.

Assumptions

The study assumes that most adolescents who are likely to enter into marital life later would desire to learn in schools and colleges about sexuality, reproductivity, mother and child care, nutrition etc. However, in the absence of what information and knowledge on the above issue are acquired already and what are their current needs, it posses a challenge to us in planning population education programmes for the students of higher secondary schools and higher education institutions.

In the above context, it is relevant to make a study on the students in schools and colleges to assess what they currently know about sexuality and reproductive activity. This assessment will help us to identify training/learning needs in population education and develop appropriate curricular approach.

Limitations

This research study has several limitations. First of all, it covers only school or college going adolescents. The real educational needs of adolescents cannot be determined unless the needs of those who are neither in school nor in college are also considered. Further the survey does not represent the rural adolescents and most institutions selected are in the urban area and a college are also considered. Further the survey does not represent the rural adolescents and most institutions selected are in the urban area and a few located in the periphery.

An attempt was, however, made to include a small group of rural adolescents. Then the survey method was found inappropriate and it required focus group discussions. Since the time at the disposal of researchers was limited, the study was limited to institutionalised survey approach.

Since the major objective of this study is to identify curriculum units/areas, the selection of respondents were restricted to schools and colleges.

References

1. World Population Plan of Action, 1994, UNFPA.
2 The State of World Population 1997, UNFPA.
3. Antony R. Measham and Richard, A. Heaver, India's Family Welfare, Moving to Reproductive and Child Health Approach (1994) and its supplement, 1996.

Chapter 4

Review of Related Studies

Introduction

A number of community health surveys have been carried out from time to time in order to discover the health status of the community. Some of these surveys are specific in their nature, approaches, target and goals. Some are detailed and general too. But many of the detailed health surveys normally include households with specific concern for the married women and their children. These hardly ever include adolescent boys and girls and little concern is shown to their education, counselling and other health problems they face and how to meet their information, education and counselling needs. It is also essential to diagnose the primary health problems of adolescents girls and boys, their unmet health needs, the need for education and counselling on vital area of concern for them so that policy directions, appropriate programs and possible solutions to problems are explored.

Before planning the study it is useful to review various surveys/ researches conducted in this area.

The National Family Health Survey 1992-93,[1] the largest ever population and health survey undertaken in our country, covered nearly 90,000 households in 24 States plus the Union Territory of Delhi. Using uniform sampling designs, field procedures and questionnaires, they interviewed 89,777 married women between the ages of 13 and 49. The data so gathered also related to their current status and their needs with regard to their health and reproductive function. This study revealed that despite intensive information, education and communication (IEC) strategies adopted for established population., we are far from achieving the goal and the reason being lack of choices or power for women to make decisions regarding their production. And empowering women, therefore, is considered a fundamental step for making them exercise their rights which include equality of opportunity for education and employment, access to resources and control of all aspects of their health and in particular their own fertility.

Nepal Family Health Survey of 1996[2] published in March 1997 is a fifth in a series of demographic and health surveys conducted in Nepal since 1976. The survey covers nationally representative sample of 8,429 ever married women aged 15-49. The study has reported a decline on the Total Fertility Rate, gradual increase in the age at marriage, yet left with persistent features of early child-bearing and short birth intervals. The study throws light on various demographic indicators of fertility, mortality, morbidity rates along with the practices of family planning methods, child rearing practices, nutritional status of children and so on.

The Young Adult Fertility and Sexuality study (YAFSII)[3] a project by UNFPA and conducted in 1994 provides information on dating, marriage and the onset of sexual activity among all young men and women aged 15-24 years in the Philippines. A total of 10,879 young people were interviewed with separate questionnaires for men and women and for married and unmarried respondents. The information emerged on marriage and sexual activities was considered as important in planning reproductive health and family planning programmes.

The survey reported that most sexual activity takes place within the context of a committed rather than a casual relationship. Premarital sex among the young men and women surveyed was found to be higher than it was found to be leading to formal marriage. This study clearly indicated the need for policy shift towards providing reproductive health information and services for unmarried youth.

A special report published in Integration by Nancy Yinger[4] describes a research study conducted by Social and Rural Research Institute (SRI) on the unmet needs for family planning in two districts of Uttar Pradesh. The study has a qualitative and a quantitative phase. SRI conducted 120 in-depth interview with women and also with their husbands and mother-in-law. This study estimates the unmet needs for family planning to be 35 per cent.

The study revealed that women have very little knowledge about marriage, sex and other reproductive health issues and thus very little grounds on which to make choices about their reproductive lives. They also have very limited or no decision making role with regard to choice of husband, when to marry, use of contraceptives etc. People in general have fear and apprehension about family planning methods and a high rate of sexual violence was also observed.

A Study was made in Hong Kong[5] on the school students show that few parents talk to their children about sex even in developed countries. Some of the studies made in Kenya[6] and Sub-Saharan Africa[7] also concur with similar results. All these go to prove that school system should take a major role in offering education in sexuality and related areas of concern to adolescent groups in the school and higher education system.

Barker and Rich[8] have studied the adolescent sexuality in Nigeria in 1990 using the methodology of focus - group discussions organized among the adolescents. The study reports that the adolescents in Nigeria learned about sexuality from popular magazines with names such as Lolly, Fantasy etc., Some young people have even mentioned learning about sex from adult movies.

African youths organisations[9] working with WHO have used an innovative "narrative method" to gather information about young adults', lives and then to plan programmes accordingly.

The narrative methods involved developing stores about a man or a women who notice each other, meet, become friendly and make decisions about their relationship. Through role playing, the participants determine how these events would take place in their culture.

Dr. Gopalan[10] has observed that adolescents have been neglected by the health services and this group has important health and information needs particularly with regard to nutrition, sexuality and reproduction. He observed that, one in four married adolescents is a mother and all married adolescents, because of their high health risk, require special attention through the package of essential services. A majority of adolescent girls, married or not are anaemic, often to moderate or severe degree'.

Studies on gender inequalities are numerous. Particularly many studies have pointed out how gender and gender inequalities are reflected in demographic processes to varying degrees and in different ways. For instance, a strong son preference in India due to higher socio-economic and cultural value ascribed, adversely affect the ratio of men to women[11, 12, 13].

In many Asian countries like India and Bangladesh, females have higher mortality rates than males at all ages even though females have greater physiological resistance to infections and diseases. This gender discrepancy can be traced to differential treatment given to boys and girls in terms of nutrition, health care and education. Tradition dictates that men and boys are served food first with less or nutritionally poor diet often only with left over to women and girls. When children contract infection and diseases, boys are taken to health clinics or physicians more often than are girls. These differences are observed even in breast-feeding practices of male and female children.

From various qualitative studies conducted in different parts of the world through focus group discussions, it has been concluded that adolescents around the world report a lack of adequate information about reproduction, sexuality, family planning and health.

Assessment studies relating to the level of knowledge, attitudes and practices related to adolescent men and women on sexuality and reproductive health are not many. In 1991, in Bolivia and in-depth study of women's reproductive health knowledge, attitudes and practices was undertaken. The study describes the population's, perceptions and behaviour in relation to the formal health care system and provides information that can be used to prepare intervention strategies aimed at improving maternal and neonatal health[14].

Mahesh Deouskar[15] has studied Population Education as perceived by teachers and students and has reported that female teachers and students of urban and rural area are more knowledgeable on population problems and population growth than their male counter parts. The study also points out that teachers and students have strong beliefs and attitude towards population education and are therefore ready to accept population education as part of the curricula.

The State Resources Centre, Uttar Pradesh, Literacy House[16], has made a study of male and female adolescents in the urban and rural areas. Most of the male adolescents are daily labourers and female adolescents are household workers. A sample of 363 adolescents was covered whose knowledge, attitude and behaviour regarding gender equality, small family norms, reproductive health and reproductive rights was assessed through discussions and interviews.

The study established that gender equality was unknown and the adolescent girls felt that they were a burden on the family, they had poorer self-image while their counterparts felt superior. The majority of learners felt that property should be inherited by sons. However, they had the understanding that education can improve their status. The preference for son was highly dominant mainly for continuing ones heredity support an care of parents and other orders. And family planning was mostly unknown to them.

A study of Awareness of Population Eduction among college students conducted by the PERC (Madras)[17] revealed that they posses lower level of knowledge in several aspects of demography, health, women's status, environment etc. Similarly another study on AIDS awareness among college students conducted by PERC (Madras)[18] indicated a higher level of awareness of HIV/AIDS which revealed that they could as well be utilised as catalyst for extension activities. These researches suggest that special counselling services coupled with education should be made available to all adolescents. And action researches and need assessments are required to be made in the areas of adolescent sexuality, health etc. so that the education system at different levels and mass media undertake adolescent education programmes including population education covering themes relevant to adolescents. Particularly reaching boys at a young age through school and college based instructions supported by well designed mass-media based programmes can be effective in shaping their attitudes and practices in later life.

In support of education on adolescent sexuality, we find several such observations. For instance studies of Bhatt[19] and Solapurkar[20] in Baroda, Bombay and sholapur respectively show that adolescents are far less likely to practice contraception than women aged 20-24 and unmarried adolescents constitute a sizable proportion of abortion seekers. They also often delay their abortions until dangerously late because or ignorance or fear of social stigmatization.

There have been a number of demographic and health surveys conducted in India and in other developing countries which are primarily concerned with fertility, mortality and migration rates. In addition a number of studies have recorded the pregnancy and contraceptive use status of women of child-bearing age. However, it appears that research studies on adolescent groups particularly assessing their educational and counselling needs and problems with regard to their sexuality and reproductive activities are scarce or absent.

References

1. National Family Health Survey (NFHS) Report, Ministry of Health and Family Welfare, 1995.
2. Report of Nepal Family Health Survey (1996), Family Health Division, Ministry of Health of His majesty's Govt. of Nepal, March 1997.
3. The Young Adult Fertility and Sexuality Study II, A Brief Report, Asia - Pacific Population Policy, East West Centre Report No. 42, July 1997.
4. Nancy Yinger, Long Term Issues, Integration, Summer 1997 vol. No. 52.
5. The Adolescents Sexuality Study, 1986. The School Survey - Family Planning Association of Hong Kong Newsletter, Vol. 58 : pp. 1-2 July, 1988.
6. Ojwang S.B.O. and Maggwa A.B.N. : Adolescents Sexuality in Kenya, East African Medical Journal 68(2) : pp. 8-74 February, 1991.
7. Gyepi - Garbarah, B. Bicholas D.J. and Kpedekpo G.M.K. Adolescent Fertility in Sub-Saharan Africa : An overview,

Boston, Pathfinder Fund 1985 reported in Population Reports, July 1996, Series - J. No. 41.

8. Barker G.K. and Rich, S., Influences on Adolescent Sexuality in Nigeria and Kenya, Findings from Focus group discussions, Studies in Family Planning Vol. 23(3), pp. 199-210 May-June 1992.
9. WHO Regional Office for Africa, Adolescent Sexual Behaviour and Reproductive Health : From Research to Action : The Narrative Research Method, Report of a Joint Meeting, Dakar, Senegal, April 22-26, 1993.
10. Gopalan, C. Nutrition in Developmental Transition on South-East Asia 1992, SEARO, Regional Health Paper 21, Regional office for South East Asia, WHO, New Delhi.
11. Radha Balakrishnan, 'The Social Context of Sex Selection and the Policies of Abortion in India': in Power and Decision in the Book the social control and Reproduction (eds.) G. Sen and R. Snow, Cambridge, Harvard University Press. 1994.
12. Lincoln Chen, Embadul Huq and Stan D'Souza, Sex Bias in the Family Allocation of Food and Health Care in Rural Bangladesh, Population and Development Review, Vol. 17(1): pp. 35-52.
13. N.I. Sabir, and G.J. Ibrahim, Are Daughters More at risk than sons in some societies? Journal of Tropical Paediatrics, August, 1994 Vol. 30 (4) : pp. 237-9.
14. USAID, Mother Care Project, Qualitative Research, Knowledge, Attitudes and Practices related to Women's Reproductive Health, Washington D.C., 1991 (from the Population Education - Accession List, July - Dec. 1995).
15. Deouskar, Mahesh, Population Education - as Perceived by teachers and Students, New Delhi, Reliance Publishing House, 1997.
16. A study of Adolescents Learners knowledge, Attitude and Behaviour Regarding Gender Equality, Small family Norms, Reproductive Health and Reproductive Rights, reported in Literacy & Population No. 9-10 Jan.-June 1998.
17. Population Education Resources Centre, Chennai A study on Awareness of Population Education among College Students, Deptt. of adult and Continuing Education, University of Madras.
18. Population Education Resources Centre, Chennai, A study on AIDS Awareness among College Students, Dept. of Adult and Continuing Education, University of Madras 1995.
19. Bhatt R.V. An Indian Study of he psycho-Social behaviour of Pregnant Teenage Women Journal of Reproductive Medicine Vol 21 : 4, 1978.
20. Solapurkar, M.L. and Sangam R.N. Has the MTP Act in India Proved Beneficial? Journal of Family Welfare, Vol. 31:3.

Chapter 5

Methodology

Reaching out to adolescence and young adults for organising population education programmes require that we need to learn more about young people's sexual activities and their needs, forced sex or premarital sex and pregnancies and their avoidance, their perceptions of sex roles, their knowledge on the methods of family planning etc.

Several surveys and research activities are hence needed to address the adolescents and young adults. Such activities will include.

— Design of strategies and methods of data collection. This is particularly difficult from adolescents who are not in the formal education system.
— Assessing the information, education, guidance and counselling services required.
— Identifying problems and needs of adolescents and young adults.
— Identify linkages between education, health, poverty and family well being.
— Establishing comprehensive and reliable qualitative and quantitative database.

Such studies will certainly facilitate and influence health and family welfare, policy formulation and legislation and help planning for delivering quality reproductive health care services to the adolescence and young adults.

It was therefore decided to undertake a survey on the

adolescence boys and girls studying in the XI and XII standards in schools and the undergraduate students of colleges in Madras city to cover a wider age range between 16-21 years.

The table below shows the number of adolescents covered in this study.

Table 5.1
Sample

Sex	*Schools (N=5)*	*Colleges (N=5)*	*G. Total*
Boys	126	137	263
Girls	238	413	651
Total	364	550	914

As the adolescent sexuality and reproductive activity are more predominant concerns of girls, more number of girls were included in the study. It was planned to cover at a ratio of 1:3 for boys and girls respectively. For want of complete information 25 questionnaire schedules were rejected. The study thus included 263 boys and 651 girls from whom basic information, on several population related areas were gathered.

Methods and Tools

A questionnaire schedule for adolescents girls and boys was prepared consisting of 18 items covering the following major areas:

1. Background data
2. Type of health care sought
3. Knowledge on family planning methods
4. Age at menarche and problems during Menstruation/ Adolescence related.
5. Source of information on adolescence/Problems of Adolescents.
6. Attitudes/knowledge on marriage, sexuality, sex education, termination of pregnancy.
7. Knowledge on pregnancy and child health/care/breast-feeding etc.
8. Age at marriage, preference of sex
9. Need for information related to health, pregnancy, child care etc.
10. HIV/AIDS.

A greater number of items on the above area focused on testing their knowledge and a few items were open-ended in nature which were included to measure there needs for information/ education on human sexuality, reproductive health and related services required by them.

Family Planning Related Content

Including family planning concepts for higher secondary school and first degree students will permit adolescents to reflect over time on the implications of family planning and inspected births. The items included in the questionnaire aimed at assessing their knowledge on these issues so that priorities are set in content areas such as family size and norm, planning the births, possible ways and means of preventing births, understanding on parenting responsibilities etc.

Family Life and Human Sexuality

Family life and human sexuality are universally important sources of content for population education. Unless the existing level of knowledge on these areas are known, it is difficult to plan the contents for teaching-learning.

Maternal Health Child Care Approach

The concepts of safe delivery, health motherhood and care of the child are important for adolescents so that they receive message that will help to improve their knowledge and modify their behaviour as related to their personal health and the health of children, thereby building readiness for responsible parenthood.

Gender Issues

Population education is not restricted to teaching learning of sexuality, reproductivity and maternal and child health but is intricately and intensely related to gender issues. This should help students to form positive attitudes and values regarding gender. These attitudes should include fairness and justice, avoidance of unhelpful/harmful stereotypes and understanding the implications of parenting.

It is strongly contended that population education planned for adolescents should go beyond a single issue approach and recognize the significance and relevance of other related issues both at the macro and micro levels. The educators should offer learners a balanced population education content that range from social demography, family life to environment and human sexuality. In validating this contention, it is believed that the present study will help to reconceptualize population education content realistically by identifying the needs and problems of adolescents with regard to acquiring knowledge on family life, sexuality, gender issues, reproductivity etc.

It was therefore planned to measure the knowledge and attitudes of students in schools and colleges in all the above stated areas.

Data Gathering

The volunteer school and college teachers many of whom happen to be Ph.D. research scholars in the Department of Adult & Continuing Education were briefed on the goals and objectives of the research study and the qeustionnaire. They were trained in the use of questionnaire prepared and the method of collecting data. The data so gathered by them is analysed and reported. The questionnaire is appended (Appendix I).

In addition, the study also included assessment of teachers, views and perceptions about adolescents behaviour with regard to sex, sex education etc. A short opinionnaire consisting of 20 items was prepared and administered. Out of 20 items was prepared and administered. Out of 20 items, some related to assessing their attitude to sex education, some related to their opinion on adolescent behaviour, some on teaching sex education, and integrating population education into the curriculum. The opinionnaire is appended (Appendix 2). 133 teachers responded to the items in the opinionnaire. The result are analysed and presented separately.

Chapter 6

Results and Discussions

Section I
Results of Teachers Opinionnaire

The opinionnaire for teachers consisted of 20 items relating to knowledge of and attitude to sex education and perceptions about sex related adolescent behaviour. 133 teachers responded to the opinionnaire.

It was not planned initially to collect the background information about the teachers - their sex and the education system to which they belong. No attempt could therefore be made to report on the basis of sex or the level (college or school) where the teachers work. And the responses of teachers to all the 20 items were pooled for the purpose of analysis.

The first two items relate to teachers' perception about adolescent behaviour. It is heartening to find a healthy and positive attitude the teachers hold towards he adolescents' sex behaviour. While only 17.3 per cent teachers consider adolescents generally to indulge in sexμal activity, there is slight increase in the percentage of teachers (26.3%) who believe that adolescents in urban areas start sex prior to marriage.

One third of the teachers who responded to the opinionnaire do not consider STD and HIV/AIDS to be posing any threat to adolescents as compared to adults. The above observation is further confirmed by the responses to an item which observes that more than 51 per cent of the teachers consider HIV/AIDS education carried on currently in schools and colleges as unfounded and baseless. More than two-thirds of the teachers feel also that men alone are not responsible for the spread of STD and HIV/AIDS.

59.4 per cent of the teachers who participated in the survey are not aware that information regarding contraceptives and free distribution of contraceptives like condoms are available freely to the students. They consider such activities as illegal.

With regard to advocating the use of condoms among adolescents, the opinions of teachers are divided equally i.e. nearly 49 per cent teachers approving and another 51 per cent not approving the advocacy for and use of condoms among adolescents.

More than 75 per cent of teachers who participated in the survey surprisingly report that they do not consider early marriage and parenthood to be a problem. This is probably due to the sample of teachers having been drawn primarily from the city of Chennai.

It is paradoxical to find that 86.5 per cent of teachers do not consider that the adolescents should receive education on human sexuality and family life education. This view is further clarified in Item 10 of the schedule in which about 76 per cent of the teachers (101 out of 133) have expressed that education on human sexuality is not the responsibility of schools and colleges. They are also of the view (nearly 80 per cent of teachers) that media should certainly not meddle with sex education for students. It is relevant to quote ORG-Marg opinion Poll, N. Delhi reported in India today. 48 percent of Indians is reported as not in favour of sex education at school level.

82.7 per cent of teachers however agree that population education should be integrated into school curriculum and with regard to integration into higher education system, the teachers are divided into 44.4 per cent agreeing and 55.6 per cent disagreeing for integration. It is really intriguing to find that while the group is not really opposing to incorporate population education both into the school and the college curriculum, they appear to be opposed to the concept of sex education or education on human sexuality. It is probably a problem of nomenclature. It is, therefore, understandable to find the group (70.7%) strongly believing that sex education for adolescents will negatively influence their morality.

With regard to an item whether adolescents learn about sex from their peer group, 85 per cent of teachers believe that the peer group influence does not exist.

Being more urban based, the teachers probably do not agree that adolescents face serious health risks for want of access to health care facilities.

However 80 per cent of the teachers agree that they require special training for teaching units on human sexuality. More than 90 per cent of the teachers agree that population education should form part of moral education also and guidance and counselling centres on sexuality and adolescent behaviour are required at the schools and colleges.

Based on the above results, the following observations are significant.

1. Overall, the teachers continue to have faith in the adolescents and consider tradition still dominating in maintaining their modesty and morality.
2. Sex education or education on human sexuality or family life education, whatever be the nomenclatures attributed, is yet to find favour and approval of teachers in school and colleges. This is corroborated by the observations and comments made and inhibitions exhibited by the teachers while collecting data from the students. Some of the items relating to sexual harassment, rape, premarital sex, masturbation, condoms etc. were therefore, forbidden. The teachers objected these terms and described questionnaire itself as 'sexy', 'insensitive', 'sensitising negatively' and so on and expressed that these affected the modesty, culture and tradition of the school'. This was more explicit in schools than in the colleges.
3. Since through items 9 and 10, teachers appear to hold a view that education of adolescents on sexuality and family life is not the function of schools and colleges, one problem that needs to be address immediately and more intensely is advocacy for teachers and bringing out clarity on issues

of population education, sex education etc. There is therefore greater need for more advocacy programmes before integrating into the curriculum and emphasise the role of schools and colleges in undertaking responsibility for eduction of adolescents on human sexuality.

Section II
Analysis of Students' Responses

The Sample

Of the 914 student respondents, the college students, covered were 350 and 364 school students were covered. The following are the sex-wise distribution of respondents.

Table 6.1

	College N = 550			*School N = 364*		
	Male	*Female*	*Total*	*Male*	*Female*	*Total*
No.	137	413	550	126	238	364
%	26.7	73.3	100%	34.6	65.4	100%

As explained earlier, it was decided to cover male and female students at the ratio of 1:3 and accordingly attempts were made. However, when the final sample emerged, it is seen that among the college students, more number of girls responded and returned the schedules than boys. There is nevertheless a higher representation of boys from the school sector. The age of respondents ranged between 16-22 years.

Retrospective Morbidity History of Adolescents

There were two items to study the retrospective history of morbidity of the adolescents. The objectives of these items were to find out 1) What is the incidence of reported morbidity during 3 months prior to the survey and 2) to whom did they refer, in other words, the type of treatment they preferred.

It is observed that only 253(out of 914) had reportedly fallen ill. Nearly 66 per cent of the students reported no occurrence of any sickness.

Of those reported ill, the table below indicates sex wise and college and school-wise distribution.

Table 6.2
Morbidity Data

	College			*School*		
	Male	*Female*	*Total*	*Male*	*Female*	*Total*
No.	34	112	146	34	73	107
%	24.8	27.2	26.5	26.8	30.7	29.3

Overall, we find a low morbidity level observed among the adolescents. There is however a slightly increased morbidity trend seen among the school students, particularly among girls.

With regard to the practice of seeking medical assistance for any illness, it is understandable that a majority of both boys and girls from schools and colleges, being drawn from the city or neighbourhood, go to private doctors only. However, 22 per cent of the sample reported either treatment at home or with Indian Medicine.

Knowledge of Adolescents on Family Planning

The knowledge of students on the permanent and temporary methods of family planning was assessed through open ended questions.

In respect of permanent methods of family planning, nearly one-third of the sample studied (32.9%) in both the school and college groups had equally not responded to this item. Tubectomy was more popular and known to many as compared to vasectomy or laparoscopy. It is intriguing to observe a higher percentage of school students (62% as against 54% of college students) knew about tubectomy. However, vasectomy was less known among the school students (3.3% as against 11.8% by college students). Between the male and female students in colleges, a higher percentage of male students (13.2%) than female students (9.7%) knew about vasectomy. In general, both the groups (college and school students) appear to be unfamiliar with laparoscopy.

With regard to temporary methods of contraception it is found that about 39 per cent of students in both groups did not respond to this item. The difference in non response in the school category was higher (47.3%) as compared to 32.9 per cent among college students. Self-control and natural methods were hardly ever mentioned by them. However, condoms and copper-T are more popularly known by the college students while only 18 per cent of the school students had mentioned these.

When the same question was put in a different way and the students were asked to report the methods of postponing or delaying child births, 41 per cent of college students and 52.4 per cent of school students wrote 'Don't know'. They probably associate condoms, Cooper T, Vasectomy, Tubectomy etc. only with limiting births and not with delaying or postponing pregnancy and these could be removed when the couples desire to have a child. This emphasises the need for developing certain conceptual clarify for them on these issues.

Information on Menstruation and Related Issues

There were 3 items meant only for girls. These related to age at maturity and problems related to menstruation.

Age at Menarche

Table 6.3
Mean age at Menarche

Institution	*Age*	*No. of Students*
College	13.32	413
School	12.86	240
Overall	13.19	653

Though the mean age at menarche for the whole group is 13.19, the age range is between 10 and 16 years. Between the ages of 10 and 11, while 11.8 percent college girls have reported to have attained menarche, this figure nearly doubles with 21.8 per cent of school girls having attained menarche. This indicates a definite declining trend in age at menarche of girls thus widening the gap between menarche and marriage and the potential threat of behavioural changes likely to manifest in this very important population sub group. The revolution in media and information technologies in exposing this vital sub group to sex-oriented knowledge, attitudes and values makes for reaching but mostly unhealthy impact on this group because these are mostly unplanned and untargetted. The changing finally structure and relationships on the one hand and the lackadaisical attitudes of teachers, parents and other elders on the other to these changing relatives further complicate the issue of education in human sexuality for the adolescents.

Menstrual Problems Reported by Adolescents

In general, a very small percentage of students reported irregular menstruation. For the college and the school group, it is 9.4 per cent and 5.2 per cent respectively having irregular periods. 41.6 per cent of the college girls (172 out of 413) and 34 per cent of school girls (81 out of 238) reported problems and feeling of sickness during menstruation. The types of problems these girls reported to have experienced are given in the following table.

Table 6,4
Menstrual Problems of Adolescents

Type of Problem	*College (N=172)*		*School (N*	*Total= 81)*		
	No.	*%*	*No.*	*%*	*No.*	*%*
1. Head Ache	11	6.4	7	8.6	18	7.1
2. Stomach Pain	141	82.0	37	45.7	178	70.3
3. Excessive bleeding	19	11.0	6	7.4	25	9.9
4. Vague or non specific symptoms like Nausea, exhaustion, dullness loss of apetite	65	37.8	17	20.9	72	88.9

As expected, the menstrual related problems appear to be normal relating to stomach pain and other related nausea, dullness, exhaustion as experienced normally by all. We may infer that the sample studied appear to be comparatively in normal health.

A question on how many of them have sought medical advice on menstrual health or for menstrual related problems, it is heartening to find a healthy practice among them. 68.7 per cent and 66.8 per cent of college and school girls respectively have at some point of time or other sought medical advice.

Preferred Source of Sex Education

The study planned to identify sources on people from whom students week with trust and confidence information on sexual matters. The list of people/sources and the preference of students are given in the table below :

Table 6.5
Preferred Sources of Sex Education

Categories	*College*			*School*		
	Great extent %	*Some extent %*	*Not at all %*	*Great extent %*	*Some extent %*	*Not at all %*
Parents	5.4	11.5	83.1	6.3	13.5	80.2
Sibligings and Relatives	8.2	10.5	81.3	5.5	13.7	80.0
Friends/Peer group	34.4	20.4	45.2	39.3	17.6	43.1
Medical Advice	29.1	16.9	54.0	22.8	15.4	66.8
Media	28.0	24.6	47.4	23.9	25.8	50.4

It is evident from the above table that there is a great deal of impact of friends being trusted and consulted on sex related matters followed by preference for medical advice. This clearly points out the need for training peer group counselling, and also creating institutional sexual health education and counselling support with the help of health professionals. The study reveals further that Media also plays and important role in educating adolescents on sexuality. This indicates the need to streamline the existing programmes, check their authenticity and relevance besides preparing appropriate programmes on sex education targeted to adolescents. And adolescents do not appear to confide with other like parents, siblings or other elders. This point demands our attention for we need to plan sex education programmes for parents and jointly with parents for the adolescents with a view to train them on counselling and guidance on adolescent sexuality. Besides parents also require help in developing rapport for being friendly and open and for building trust with their adolescent wards.

Between the school and the college, more or less similar trend is observed, although there is less dependence on media or preference to seek medical advice as compared to peer group influence.

In order to see whether there is any sex difference observed with regard to seeking information on sex or discussing problems related to sexuality analysis of only one category of response 'Not at all' was considered. This is presented below :

Table 6.6
Sex-wise Not Preferred Source of Sex Education

Categories	*College*		*School*	
	Male	*Female*	*Male*	*Female*
Parents	82.5	83.3	92.9	73.5
Siblings and Relatives	71.5	79.7	84.1	82.4
Firneds/Peer group	20.4	53.5	22.2	54.2
Medical Advice	38.7	59.1	63.5	60.9
Media	24.1	55.4	45.2	52.9

Sex difference is observed with respect to the friends/Peer group and the media among both the groups - Schools and Colleges. Particularly friends/Peer group appear to be influencing less on girls as compared to boys. Similarly, media appear to create less impact on girls than on boys.

Preferred Source for Sex Education

How do adolescents desire to have access to sex education? It is through schools or through text books or through media - T.V. Radio and reading materials? These items brought out the following observations. More than 55 per cent of the school and college students favoured inclusion of sex education as part of the curriculum in the school and expressed that it should find a place in the text books. Nearly one-fourth of them did not have any opinion on these. With regard to sex education through media, the following observations are significant. (see Table 6.7

It is evident that sex education through media does not

enjoy much popularity among college students. Though the reasons for disapproval have not been gathered, we may probably infer that it fails to gain approval of parents and elders and/or lacks clarity.

Table 6.7
Student's Opinion on Sex Education Through Media

Sex education through media	*College*			*School*		
	Male %	*Female* %	*Total* %	*Male* %	*Female* %	*Total* %
Favoured	32.8	27.4	28.7	50.8	30.7	37.7
Not flavoured	47.5	40.4	42.2	27.0	46.6	39.8
No opinion	19.7	32.2	29.1	22.0	22.7	22.5
Total	100.0	100.0	100.0	100.0	100.0	100.0

With regard to any past history of complaints of infections in the sexual organs like itching, boils, ulcer etc. only 9.5 per cent of college girls and 14.7 per cent of school girls responded in the affirmative and have consulted doctors. More than 60 per cent of the respondents did not respond to this item probably due to their modesty and family restraint.

Adolescent's Attitude to Marriage, Premarital Sex and Sex Education

There were 9 items testing the adolescents' attitude to marriage, sex and sex education.

The colleges and schools selected for data collection predominantly draw their students from middle class and some from upper middle class. This being so, it was assumed that most students will be traditional in their outlook. As expected 25-30 per cent of the respondents preferred to remain neutral to items on sex and sex education.

Attitude to Premarital Sex

While nearly one-third of all respondents did not express any opinion on this, more females were against premarital sex. The following table indicate the respondents' attitude to premarital sex.

Though between the college and school students, there appears to be attitutional homogeneity, there is a decreasing trend among college girls in their disapproval of premarital sex as observed by the figures. 71.0 per cent of school students and 60.5 per cent of college students disapprove premarital sex.

Table 6.8
Attitude of Students to Premarital Sex

Premarital Sex	*College*			*School*		
	Male %	*Female* %	*Total* %	*Male* %	*Female* %	*Total* %
Approval	15.3	8.2	10.0	12.7	9.6	10.3
Disapproval	56.2	60.5	59.4	51.6	71.0	61.4
No opinion	28.5	31.2	30.6	35.7	19.3	28.3
Total	100.0	100.0	100.0	100.0	100.0	100.0

The above information is further clarified by two subsequent items on their attitude to premarital sex for males and females separately as indicated in the following table.

Table 6.9
Premarital Sex for Males and Females

Premarital Sex	*College*			*School*		
	Male %	*Female* %	*Total* %	*Male* %	*Female* %	*Total* %
Permitted for Male	13.9	13.1	13.3	19.1	11.3	13.6
Permitted for females	19.7	5.1	8.7	17.5	14.7	11.5

Though the group of adolescents favouring experimentation with premarital sex is very small. Yet they become probably risk prone to STD/HIV/AIDS etc. and therefore justify the need for organisation sex education and counselling in school and colleges.

Attitude to Premarital Sex and Types of Marriage

It was assumed that with increase in the level of education, their outlook on premarital sex, marriage etc. would change appreciably towards modernity and leniency.

Type of Marriage Preferred

There were three Independent items to measure their attitude to the type of marriage the students would prefer. The responses of students were categorised into 'prefer' not preferred' and 'no opinion'. A comparison of responses marked against the there categories showed agreement and therefore only the percent students who 'preferred' to different marriage types are presented in the following table.

Table 6.10
Students Preference to Type of Marriage

Premarital Sex	*College*			*School*		
	Male %	*Female* %	*Total* %	*Male* %	*Female* %	*Total* %
Arranged Marriage	48.1	69.5	64.2	41.3	60.5	60.1
Love Marriage	54.8	25.7	32.9	37.3	20.5	30.3
Joint Decision (Self + Parent)	84.7	87.2	86.5	79.4	85.7	85.3

Though arranged marriage, in general, find favour with college and school students, there is appreciable sex differences by less number of females favouring love marriage and correspondingly more females expressing in favour of arranged marriage.

There is also similar difference between the school and the college students. College students are noticeably becoming less traditional than school students. These results confirm our initial assumption that with education, outlook on premarital sex, marriage, etc. undergoes appreciable change.

Knowledge of Students on Abortion

There were two items to test the knowledge of students on abortion and the third item related to the ethics of abortion.

It surprising to find that school and college students are not fully aware that abortion is currently legalised. But of 924, 655 students (71.66%) distributed equally among schools and collages are of the opinion that abortion is illegal. With regard to an item on the safe period within which termination of pregnancy can be effected, the following results are observed.

Table 6.11

Safe Period for Termination of Pregnancy

Responses	*College*			*School*		
	Male	*Female*	*Total*	*Male*	*Female*	*Total*
Wrong	88.3	92.7	91.6	73.8	89.8	88.5
Correct	11.7	7.3	8.4	26.2	10.9	11.5

It is evident that most of them are ignorant about abortion practices. Being in the critical adolescent age and prone to risks, knowledge on safe termination of pregnancy, abortion laws etc. are vital to college students and higher secondary students.

With regard to their attitude to abortion, the analysis of data indicated support to abortion for terminating pregnancy.

Age at Marriage and Child Birth

In general, almost everyone has correctly responded the age at marriage for male and female as 21 and 18 respectively though a small number in the school have reported wrongly. The responses of students regarding desirable gap between the marriage and the first child birth are presented in the following table sex-wise and college-school wise.

Table 6.12

Spacing Between Marriage and First Child

No. of years gap	*College*			*School*			*Overall*
	Male	*Female*	*Total*	*Male*	*Female*	*Total*	
1 year	46.7	59.1	47.6	26.2	46.7	37.7	48.7
2 years	38.7	33.7	41.2	45.2	31.8	35.9	39.2
3 years	14.6	7.2	11.2	28.6	21.4	26.4	12.1

One of two years gap between the marriage and the arrival of the first child is preferred by most students and no difference in the preference is observed between the college and school students, Nearly half of the female adolescents covered in this study prefer early child birth - a year's gap after marriage - as compared to their male counter parts. The probable reason could be to complete the maternal obligations like child birth and the associated responsibilities like bearing and caring of children.

Knowledge of Students on Maternal and Child Health

How much of knowledge the adolescents, who will be the perspective mothers very soon, have acquired on areas related to maternal and child health? There were eight items provided in the questionnaire to test the knowledge of students on maternal and child health. Performance on six of these items were scored (the maximum score being 6) and the mean scores obtained by the school and college students being 3.2 and 3.6 respectively indicate that there is greater scope for improving their knowledge on these areas. It is therefore necessary to include teaching learning content on material and child health progressively for the school and college students.

As compared to school students, college students have acquired more knowledge and between the sexes, females appear to have gained better knowledge than males. The man differences in knowledge in the areas of maternal and child health was statistically tested (using 't' test) between the college and school students (table 6.13), between males and females (table 6.14), between the college males and school males (table 6.17). The justification for doing this analysis is to show the gender bias prevalent among the boys who probably consider acquisition of knowledge on maternal and child health as one of female related. These tables are presented below :

Table 6.13
Mean Difference in Knowledge Between College and School Students

Category	*Mean*	*SD*	*'T' value*	
College (N=415)	3.6200	1.337	4.37	Significant
School (N=241)	3.2335	1.289		

There is significant differences between the school and college students with regard to knowledge attained by them. The college students have increased knowledge as compared to school students.

Table 6.14
Mean Differences in Scores Between Sexes

Category	*Mean*	*SD*	*'T' value*	
Male (N=258)	3.1434	1.308	4.67	Not Significant
Female (N=656)	3.5930	1.319		

Between the male and female adolescents, the female students have significantly increased knowledge than males.

Table 6.15
Mean Difference in Scores Between College Males and School Males

Category	*Mean*	*SD*	*'T' value*	
College (N=135)	3.0593	1.549	1.16	Not Significant
School (N=123)	3.2439	0.978		

The observation found in Tables 6.13 and 6.14 are confirmed by the results obtained in Table 6.15. There is no significant difference in the knowledge attained by the males in schools and colleges.

Table 6.16
Mean Difference in Score Between College Female and School Female

Category	*Mean*	*SD*	*'T' value*	
College Female (N=415)	3.8024	1.208	5.26	Significant
School Male (N=241)	3.2282	1.424		

Similarly there is significant difference between the college and school female students.

Table 6.17
Mean Difference in Scores Between Sexes in the School

Category	*Mean*	*SD*	*'T' value*	
College Female (N=123)	3.2439	0.978	0.12	Not Significant
School Male (N=241)	3.2282	1.424		

There is no significant difference in the knowledge of school students between sexes.

Both the college and school students lack information on various immunizations to be provided during infancy. Small box and Polio vaccines along are known to most students (80%). The reasons probably are that this group is not immediately concerned about infant care and diseases and therefore has not bothered to learn about even from different media.

Marriages and Reproductive Rights

More than 85 per cent of both boys and girls are well aware of the consequence of early marriage.

The questionnaire contained two items on reproductive rights such as

i) who should determine when to beget a child
ii) who should take responsibility for child care and
iii) one item on sex preference

The analysis of above responses brought out the following results.

It is observed that more than 95 per cent of the college students - equally similar between - sexes consider that it should be the right of the wife to decide when to conceive a child. It is surprising to find only three (1 male 2 male) students consider it as a joint responsibility. On the contrary, the views of school students differ widely. While 93 per cent of boys in schools consider that the in-laws and other elders should have a major say on this issue, the girls appear to differ in their views. While 63 per cent of the girls in schools consider it as their right, another 33.5 per cent consider it as right of in-laws and other elders.

With regard to the responsibility of child care, there is high level of agreement among the adolescents both from the colleges and the schools. There is also no difference observed between the sexed. Child care is considered to be the joint responsibility of husband and wife. This indicates a shift in the attitude to parental role among the younger generation.

Sex Preference

The preference of adolescents with regard to the sex of their first child, it is heartening to find from Table 6.18 the disappearance of gender bias among the adolescents.

Table 6.18
Sex Preference of Adolescents

	Preference category	*College*		*School*		*Overall*
		Male	*Female*	*Male*	*Female*	
1.	Male	9.5	7.7	8.7	16.0	10.3
2.	Female	5.1	3.4	2.4	5.5	4.0
3.	No Preference any six acceptable	83.2	87.4	88.1	76.9	84.1
4.	Not responded	2.2	1.5	0.8	1.7	1.5

The Reasons for Preference of Sons

Why do people desire to have sons? Opinions may widely differ between fulfilling the desire for procreating male heirs, or desire to give and receive or a source of income and so on.

So far, our conception is that sons are source of income in two ways. In the economic sense, they contribute or add to the family income and also bring money in the form of dowry, while daughters are looked upon as liability. In the social and traditional context, sons are essential to perform the last rites of parents and still continue to enjoy the right of inheritance and are also considered to continue the family lineage. How are the adolescents have moved away from the traditional ideatum?

In order to find answers to the above questions, nine probable reasons were listed and the adolescent respondents were asked to rank them in the order of their preference. The result are indicated below.

Table 6.19
Rank Order of Reasons for Son Preference

Reason for son Preference	*Rank*	*Percent*	*respondents who ranked*
1. Show/receive love	1	68.4	
2. Develop lineage/ through sons only	2	45.8	
3. Perform last rites	8	35.1	
4. Protect property	6	37.9	Another 16.2% respondents ranked this item as 5th
5. Old age support	9	32.5	Another 16.2% accorded 7th rank to this item
6. Help in work/ profession	4	40.1	
7. Companionship	7	35.7	
8. Source of added income	3	43.6	
9. Get dowry	5	38.8	34.2% ranked it as 6th
10. Pride of producing male heir	10	32.1	16.2% ranked it as 9th

Though we find major attitudional change in the adolescent group with regard to the traditional beliefs and concepts like old age support, performance of last rates, pride of producing male heir, yet, there is greater scope for bringing about changes in their attitudes. We find that lineage traced through sons only, source of increase in the income through help in work/profession and dowry still dominate. It is clear that we have to come a long way and it is only a gradual change in the attitudes of adolescent is possible if concerted efforts are made to educate them on the gender bias practiced in the society.

AIDS Awareness of Adolescents

Items testing the knowledge of adolescent on HIV/AIDS carried a total score of 10 and the scores obtained by them are given below.

Table 6.20
Knowledge on HIV/AIDS of Adolescents

Description	*College*		*School*		*Overall*
	Male	*Female*	*Male*	*Female*	
Mean scores	9.40	9.56	9.84	9.70	9.77

A very high mean score of both the groups - college and school ranging between 9.4 to 9.7 indicate a very high level of knowledge on AIDS among the adolescents.

Source of Knowledge of Pregnancy, and Related Matters

Whatever knowledge the adolescent currently possesses as on pregnancy and related matters from what sources, these have been gained?

The sources were classified under the following broad categories.

1. Friends and peer groups
2. Parents and other elders, siblings etc.
3. Medical / health personnel
4. Media like TV, Radio and print materials
5. Any other

The adolescents were asked to mark to what extent they obtain knowledge from these sources. Only the responses in the category of 'to great extent' for each of the sources are given below. Therefore the total will not add upto 100 per cent.

It is clear from the table that friends and peer group make a greater impact for male adolescent in the colleges than their female counterparts or even the adolescent from schools. As encouraging phenomena observed here relates to the influence of medical/ health personnel as a major source of knowledge as evidenced in the overall percentage (46.9%) and also the adolescent of colleges and schools.

Table 6.21
Most Preferred Source of Knowledge of Pregnancy, Termination of Pregnancy and Birth Control

S.No.	*Category*	*College*		*School*		*Overall*
		Male	*Female*	*Male*	*Female*	
1.	Friends and peer group	62.0	25.7	42.9	30.7	34.8
2.	Parents & other elders including siblings	8.0	11.1	7.1	15.1	11.2
3.	Medical/Health personnel	54.7	47.2	38.9	46.2	46.9
4.	Media	51.1	30.0	35.7	33.6	34.9

Media Appears to Influence Less Among Girls than Boys.

An analysis of responses regarding 'Not preferred' source confirm the observations made earlier in Table 6.20. Table 6.21 describes the status of 'not preferred' sources.

Table 6.22
Not Preferred Source of Knowledge of Pregnancy and Related Matters

S.No.	*Category*	*College*		*School*		*Overall*
		Male	*Female*	*Male*	*Female*	
1.	Friends and peer group	10.9	20.6	10.3	25.2	18.9
2.	Parents & other elders including siblings	45.6	39.7	50.8	41.2	41.1
3.	Medical/Health personnel	12.4	15.3	17.5	24.4	17.5
4.	Media	7.3	15.7	5.1	18.5	15.1

It is evident, that parents, elders and siblings are not preferred by a large group of adolescents and comparatively more female adolescents do not prefer media as reference source on matters relating to pregnancy, termination of pregnancy and birth control.

Healthy Sexuality

The average age of marriage has risen in many parts of our country, particularly higher in urban areas. This has put young people at greater risk of having pre-marital sex often induced through the strong social and peer group pressures. Moreover, some features of modern life, specially in the co-educational institutions at the higher secondary and college levels, may increase both the desire and opportunity for premarital sex activity. The mass media further strengthen this trend.

A lack of knowledge on healthy sexuality or worse even sexual violence and coerciaon can lead to serious health consequences including frequent abortions, unintended pregnancies and STDs besides inflicting socio-psychological injuries to individuals.

In order to assess the students', understanding on what is rape, sexual abuse and masturbation, open ended questions were given. With regard to the description of both the terms (rape and sexual abuse) no discrimination was made between them by the students. However, the analysis of responses to the above question revealed the following information. Some of the statements revealed students' ignorance. Some of the students described them in scientific terms, some were emotional outbursts impinging on tradition and morality and quite a large number have either not responded or have directly expressed as 'don't know'.

A wide range of statements varying between forcibly or compulsorily touching the girl's body anywhere without consent, affecting the modesty of a girl, molestation of a girl, attacking the girl physically, making the girl nude, inability of a man to control his sex urge, animal behaviour and behaving against accepted norms and so on indicated lack of clarity on these issues. All the responses were classified under the heads 1) Vague 2) clear 3) refused to answer 4) Don't know and 5) left blank.

Table 6.23
Responses of Boys and Girls on Raping and Sexual Abuse

		College Students		School Students		Total	
S.No.	Description	No.	%	No.	%	No.	%
1.	Vague	90	22.80	166	31.70	256	27.9
2.	Clear	148	37.60	117	22.40	265	28.9
3.	Refused to answer	9	2.30	1	0.20	10	1.1
4.	Don't know	51	12.90	69	13.20	120	13.1
5.	Not filled	96	24.40	170	32.50	266	29.0
		394	100.00	523	100.00	917.00	100.00

It is evident from the Table above that about 37.3 per cent and 45.7 per cent of school and college students respectively who have not responded to this item or responded as 'Don't know' are probably either did not desire to respond or really did not know the meaning of rape and sexual abuse or were instructed by the teachers to over look these items.

However, as compared to school students, more college students appears to be aware of the meaning of these terms.

Masturbation was considered as sin by more than 80 per cent of the adolescent girls while 60 per cent of the adolescent boys reported it as normal.

Another open-ended question related to knowledge/information the school and college students desired on human sexuality and reproductive health. They were also asked to indicate associated services required by them relating to reproductive health. These items brought out the following information.

All the responses on students on human sexuality and reproductive health were classified under 8 different heads as indicated in the table below with the corresponding number of respondents.

It is puzzling to find that nearly three fourths of the school and college students participated in the survey (item 6 and 7) were either not interested in learning about human sexuality or did not know what to ask for. This phenomena is more predominant among school students than students from colleges. About 14 per cent responses showed that the students were not keen to know anything on human sexuality from teachers and would prefer to learn either from their mothers or doctors. It is further evident that only 25 per cent of the students indicated ares of knowledge/information they desired to know.

Table 6.24
Students Responses on Knowledge Desired

S.No.	*Response category*	*School*	*College*	*Total*
1.	Sex education (Knowledge on sexual intercourse, pregnancy, marriage conception related)	22	38	60
2.	Reproductive health	39	35	74
3.	Child growth, child care, Nutrition etc.	15	06	21
4.	General health matters	38	33	71
5.	STD/HIV/AIDS/Drugs/Alcohol	0	05	05
6.	Don't want to know or want to know only from mother or doctor	67	64	131
7.	Not filled in or Don't know	360	199	559
8.	Know already	0	09	09
		541	389	930

Some of the questioning raised by college students on human sexuality non of whom are married, indicate openness and eagerness to learn provided these are learnt in privacy as indicated by them.

Some of the questions raised by the students are reproduced below.

1. What is safe sex ? With wife and with others?
2. Different postures in intercourses that can be safely practiced.
3. What is healthy sex life? How many sexual intercourse are permitted during a day/week ? With what frequency?
4. How safe are the contraceptives like condom? How to examine their safety?
5. After how many intercourse a girl becomes pregnant ?

7. When is abortion safe? Should both partners agree? Why?
8. Is sexual intercourse during pregnancy safe?
9. What is wrong with love marriage? Why parents object to it? Why can't they be educated?
10. Does the appropriate age for girls to beget a child vary? How to find out?
11. What are the means and methods of safe delivery? How to ensure safe delivery?
12. How does the foetus grow into a child - Interested to know the entire process from the intercourse to foetus and child growth.
13. Is pregnancy harmful to health?
14. If good health is maintained, what is wrong with more pregnancies?
15. What are the different protective sexual intercourse methods but easy to practice without resulting in pregnancy.
16. How the sex of the child is determined?
17. What are the causes of abortion and how to prevent it?

With regard to the open-ended question on what services are required for improving their knowledge on human sexuality and reproductive health, many students did not respond. Only 129 students, 82 college students and 47 from the schools have responded to this item. Looking at their responses, some of them were found to be not directly relevant to the educationals system. However, more than one hundred of these responses clearly indicated the need for providing personal counselling services. It was observed that there were quite a large number of students and the parents including the community for improving family relations between spouses, in laws, marriage counselling services etc. Another important services desired by the students related to health care and environmental improvement, health check up etc. All the responses could be classified under 3 major heads :

1. Education and Counselling Services
2. Referral and Corrective Services
3. Community Extension services

I. Educational and Counselling Services

i) More population education programmes in schools, colleges and in the community.

ii) Counselling centre providing education and guidance on family life education for improved family relationship between spouses and in-laws; marriage counselling including knowledge on STD/HIV/AIDS; education programmes for changing male attitudes to family, child birth, care of home etc.; role of husbands for healthy and happy married life; motherhood and child care and child health etc.

iii. Teaching and training students and the community on waste management, pollution and pollution control methods.

iv. Teaching physical exercise, yoga and meditation and moral education in all educational institutions to prevent premarital sex relations.

v. Demonstrative field level exposures and through mass media, educate students

vi. School/College health curricula mass media campaigns, and health and family welfare training.

II. Referral and Corrosive Services

i. Establishing health clinics in all schools and colleges

ii. Conduct of health check-ups diagnosis and treatment of simple ailments; nutritional supplementation - either free or subsidised for and distribution of medicines, vitamins, iron, minerals etc. - to protect the health of students.

iii. Diagnosis and referral services for more complex cases.

iv. Improvement in general hygiene provision of clear drinking water hygienic toilets in the schools and colleges.

v. Development and disseminating of guidelines on risk assessment and counselling for premarital sex, use of condoms, unwanted pregnancies, abortions, STD/AIDS detection regular blood examinations etc.

III. Community extension services

i. Collaborating with community centres and NGOs for delivery of health and hygiene services to the community

ii. Conducting door-to-door campaigns on sex education, AIDS awareness, family welfare programmes, blood donation camels etc.

iii. Screening of films and discussions (though Mass Media) on human sexuality and relationships and reproductive health matters for removing misunderstandings.

Misapprehensions and for clarification of ideas.

iv. Involvement of parents and the community members in the implementation of population education.

v. Integrating health services with adult education programmes in the community.

vi. Development of parents and community groups for facilitating health care provisions and protection.

Chapter 7

Reflective Perspectives and Conclusive Comments

Over the last five decades since Independence, Indian Women have made considerable gains in areas such as education, employment and health. There is growing awareness that progressive development on women's social and economic front is primarily in the hands of women. International Conferences, particularly the UN Conference on Population and Development (CPD) held in Cairo in 1994 followed by the UN Fourth World conference on women held in 1995 in Beijing have generated greater enthusiasm for exerting towards achieving women's progress and equality.

Though the concept of reproductive health has been in existence for long, it has acquired a new meaning based on World Health Organisation (WHO) definition of general health. Reproductive health has been defined at the ICPD as a "state of complete physical, mental and social well-being and not merely the absence of disease or infirmity in all matters relating to the reproductive system and to its functions and processes". Therefore, this definition virtually includes sexual health and the provision of related health services.

According to ICMR reproductive health is package which includes safe motherhood, fertility regulation, prevention and management of reproductive tract infection, STD/HIV/AIDS and preventing complications of abortions. It is therefore related to developing ability toregulate fertility, assuring the right to determine reproductive role and functions, ensure optimal conditions for safely fulfilling biological reproductive role, handle their sexuality with dignity and responsibility, to cope with reproductive ill health and provide infertility and safe abortion services. There is a wide spectrum of issues that could be identified and related to reproductive might as such as population and development policies violence against women, control of fertility, sexuality, maternal health, mobility, abortion etc.

Issues relating of Reproductive health has conventionally been associated with women and therefore adolescent reproductive health has failed to gain significant attention. The young girls constitute 22 per cent of India's population and greater attention is to be given to the reproductive health of young girls in a country like our because they are the future mothers who will not be able to take care of their own needs but in consequence will also take care of the needs of others.

A very large group of young people aged 10-24 years are being inadvertently left off unattended, and un-serviced by health or education sectors. The adolescent behaviour is becoming a matter of grave concern due to rapid change effected as a result of urbanization, media explosion, changing family structures and consequent breakdown of adult influence on adolescents. Concern about the adolescent sexual behaviour continues to increase with the emergence of STD, HIV/AIDs...There is, on the one hand, risk of premarital and unprotected sexual activity, unwanted pregnancies and unsafe termination of pregnancies etc. among adolescent girls. On the other, there is widely prevalent practice of early marriage and early child bearing.

The adolescents therefore essentially need education, counselling and sexual health services. There are however stiff oppositions, social inhibitions and ignorance on matters related to education on human sexuality. The curriculum at the school or at the undergraduate levels hardly ever attempt to provide knowledge or skills related to human sexuality in a meaningful way. Whatever little attempts made to advocate for sex education are sporadic, inadequate and could reach only a limited group of students.

The current study attempted to measure what is the attitude of teachers to adolescents and how far do they support advocacy for population education in schools and colleges and are ready to integrate it into the curriculum.

It was encouraging to find teachers welcoming the integration of population education into the curriculum. The survey also indicated the need for increased advocacy among the teachers to develop more positive attitude and conceptual clarity regarding population education sex education, family life education and so on. This study primarily aimed at assessing the knowledge of adolescents in population education including sex education, health, child care etc. from what sources they desire to learn about human sexuality, their opinions on and attitudes to marriage, child birth, knowledge on controlling and avoiding births, abortion etc., reasons for son preference, what knowledge and services they desire to obtain regarding marriage, child birth, child care etc.

Of the 914 students respondents covered by the survey 550 students were from colleges and 364 were from schools. The male female ratio of students covered was 1:3. The age of adolescent ranged between 16-22 years.

In general, all the adolescent students were in good health as observed by retrospective history of morbidity.

It was observed that the adolescents' knowledge on family planning methods and child care was very limited indicating the need for inclusion of these untis into the curriculum.

The influence of peer group and friends was found to be dominant on the adolescent emphasizing the need for training health education and counselling support with the help of professionals. Since media also was found to play an important role, it is evident that not only new and appropriate programmes targeted to adolescent are required but the existing ones have also to be reviewed and revised.

Since adolescents do not appear to confice with elders, parents also require counselling and education on adolescent sexuality, training for developing rapport and building trust with their adolescent wards.

College students are observed to be noticeably less traditional than school students and the assumption that with education outlook on premarital sex, marriage etc. undergoes appreciable change in confirmed.

More than 55 per cent of the adolescents covered favoured including of sex education as part of curriculum and should expressed that it should find a place in the text books.

The knowledge of adolescents tested in the areas of pregnancy, child birth, family planning method, child care and health etc. indicate that there is greater scope for improving their knowledge on these areas.

When the adolescents' attitudes to 'preference for sons' was measured, it revealed the need for education them on the illogicality of the gender bias practised in society.

It was heartening to find a high level of awareness on STD/ HIV/AIDS among the adolescents.

With regard to open ended items on education and counselling services required in the areas of human sexuality and reproductive health as desired by the adolescents only a small minority (14%) of them responded meaningfully and suggestively.

They pointed out the need for family life education for both the students and the parents including the community for improving family relations and marriage counselling. Teaching and training the students and the community on environmental issues like waste management, pollution, health and family welfare was emphasised.. Besides, operating counselling centres in the colleges and extending the services to the community was also emphasised. Teaching physical exercises, yoga and mediation and moral education were reported as important components of curriculum in the schools and colleges.

Establishing health clinics in all schools and colleges, conduct of health check-ups, referral services, improvement in general hygience etc. were considered essential.

The adolescents also recognized the importance of community extensions services as part of population education.

Considering the needs of adolescents for education and counselling on human sexuality relating to biological, psychological, socio-cultural and moral dimensions, it is necessary to develop and incorporate appropriate curriculums units into the school and undergraduate curricula, prepare a wide range of learning materials like manuals, handbooks, teachers guides etc. These resource materials will serve as practical guides primarily for teachers, trainers, guidance counsellors and peer group leaders who are engaged in teaching, training and guiding adolescent students on issues concerned with adolescent growth, development and related problems,.

The study shows that adolescents lack clarity on sexual behaviour, physical, emotional and psychological changes that occur during puberty and physiological processes of human conceptions.

At the conceptual level, there is still a high level of sex stereotyping and the adolescent boys and girls are fixed in their ideas on sex roles and role expectations. Therefore they require education for changing their attitudes of sex roles, role expectations and role performance.

The adolescent education should therefore aim at making the school and undergraduate students acquire knowledge, skills and values which will prepare them for later adult life, for effective performance of their roles in marriage, parenthood, and community life and thus enable them to enjoy a quality life.

Chapter 8

Epilogue
Women Empowerment and Reproductive Rights

Our national goal and efforts towards reaching the goal of improving the status of women have always aimed at making women economically strong and independent. Women have a right to be treated with dignity and fairness. To facilitate this, women have to be integrated into the mainstream of the economy through provision of equity and social justice in education, and employment.

The low status of women in India is clearly indicated by several factors such as

- Declining sex ratio
- Lower expectancy of life at birth
- Higher infant mortality and maternal mortality
- Practice of female infancide and foeticide
- Low female work participation
- Illiteracy and poor enrolment at all levels of education
- High drop out of girls from primary to higher education levels
- High fertility rates and frequent child births
- Low age at marriage and at first pregnancy/child birth
- Poor health care and nutrition from childhood to adulthood.

Give the choice, women would rather prefer to marry late,

have fewer children - one or two participate in economic activities more fruitfully and productively, earn and become economically self-reliant.

No doubt much of our health and family welfare programme implemented in the past have brought about significant positive changes in many areas like increased expectation of life at birth, reduction in fertility levels, maternal and infant mortality, increased provision for girls' education, training and improved access to input and productive resources for women and so on.

Over the last several decades women around the world have made significant gains in several areas such as health, work and education. Since the 1960s, participation of women in the workforce has increased to 54 percent from 33 percent. Literacy rates for women have changed since the 1970s from 54 percent to 64 percent. And since the 1980s, the gap between girls and boys enrolled in all levels of education has been narrowing down significantly (Women of our World, Pop. Ref. Bureau, 1998).

Since the social status of women is deep rooted in the culture and tradition of our community, the conservative notion that a women solely belongs to her more has blocked women's progress considerably in India. Thus confining women to home alone and condemning her to a life of drudgery and stagnation is not only unfair but impedes national progress.

Sustainable women development is possible only if girls and women are educated on gender issues. Adolescents specifically require education on gender issues so that health attitudes are developed from an early age, preferably from the primacy school. More attention should be paid to avoid braiding of sex specific roles so that changes in sex role performance are accepted with ease and practised unreluctantly. This will develop a holistic approach to gender issues. Women's empowerment is attitanable only if both boys and girls (men and women) attempt to perform any role without discrimination.

There is ample evidence established on the links between gender inequality and poverty, and illiteracy, high fertility and poor health of women. Adolescent reproductive health should receive special attention boih from the health sector and education sector.

The reproductive and child health (RCH) programmes being implemented currently by our National Government at the Centre and the Governments at the States aim at providing relevant services and upgrading the level of facilities for regulating fertility, extending quality care of maternal and child health and improving the community access to RCH services besides information, education and communication strategies for adult women. However what is most important is education for adolescents on population, family life, reproductive and child health so that there is physical and mental and mental readiness among them for healthy parenthood and family life.

Population education has to be reconceptualised to emphasise education of girls and its relation to fertility, the re-examination of sex education, how to introduce education on human sexuality effectively in schools, in out of school programmes, youth programmes and in parent education and in training the service providers, to determine what topics to include and how to minimise or prevent controversies.

Population education for adolescents should emphasise inter-disciplinarity as an effective means of dealing with development problems. It should focus on sustainable development, diversity of life, building of human capacities, human dignity and rights, effective communication and provision of quality education for all. It should also address issues of emerging concerns such as aging, HIV/AIDS/STDs, reproductive rights and health, gender inequality, increasing incidence of violence on women, social evils like dowry and forced marriage, family disintegration and divorce, migration, value degeneration and so on.

ANNEXURE 1

A Schedule for Teachers

Knowledge and Perceptions About Adolescents' Behaviour

Kindly answer the following questions

1. Today adolescents start sex much younger than previous generations. True/False
2. Many adolescents in the urban areas are having sex before marriage than it was in the past. True/False
3. For adolescents, STDs, & HIV/AIDS pose more risk than for adultsrue. True/False
4. Men are primarily responsible for STDs and HIV/AIDS in Women. True/False
5. Early parenthood is still a problem in Tamilnadu True/False
6. Low prohibit or limit providing contraceptives, services or even information to adolescents. True/False
7. Advocating the use of condoms among adolescents is not desirable. True/False
8. Premarital sex is permissible, if the young adults are protected True/False

9. Education on sexuality and family life is essential for adolescents. True/False

10. The responsibility of educating adolescents on sexuality and family life should rest on the schools and college. True/False

11. HIV/AIDS Education carried on now in schools and college is unfounded and baseless. True/False

12. Most young people learn about sex from their peer groups. True/False

13. Sex Education for adolescent will negatively influence their morality. Agree/Disagree

14. Teachers require special training for teaching sexuality. Agree/Disagree

15. Adolescents face serious health risk for they have little access to health care. True/False

16. The best way to reach adolescents for sex education is through media. True/False

17. Population Education should be integrated into school curriculum. Agree/Disagree

18. Population Education should be integration only at the higher education level. Agree/Disagree

19. Guidance and counselling centres on sexuality and adolescent behaviour are required at the scl ools and colleges. Agree/Disagree

20. Population Education should form part of moral education. True/False

ANNEXURE - II

English Version of the Questionnaire for Students
University of Madras Department of Adult & Continuing Education

1. Students Background — Name of the School/College & Address

   (i) Identification Code
   (ii) Class
   (iii) Age
   (iv) Sex : Boy/Girl

2. During the last 3 months, did you fall sick and have medical check up? Yes/No

a) If Yes, to whom? b) For what problem(s)

   (i) Private nursing home/hospital/Dr.
   (ii) Govt. Hospital
   (iii) Indian medicine
   (iv) Any other

3. What are the different methods of preventing child birth?
   Permanent methods Temporary methods

4. Mention the different methods used for postponing child births?

5. (Only for Girls)
   Menarche/menstrual related problems
   (i) age at menarche Yes/No.

(ii) Is your periods regular? Yes/No
(iii) Do you have problems associated with periods Yes/No
(iv) If yes, what are they? (1) headache
(2) Stomach pain
(3) excessive bleeding
(4) nausea/giddiness
(5) week/tired/loss of apatite
(6) any other, specify

(v) Do you/did you consult the Director for the above problems? Yes/No

6. If/When you desire to learn about human sexuality/Sex education, whom do you prefer to approach?

Source	*To a great extent*	*To some extent*	*Not at all*
Parents & other elders			
Siblings			
Friends			
Medical/para medical personal			
Print Media			
Radio & TV			
Others, specify			

7. Did you/Do you have any infections/disease in sex organs (exculceration itching, while discharges etc. or any other Yes/No

(i) If yes, did you get treatment? for What problems? Yes/No

8. What are your opinions regarding the following items?

	Agree	Don't agree	No opinion
(i) There is nothing wrong in having experience in premarital sex			
(ii) Men Can have freedom in sexual matters			
(iii) Women should protect her chastity till marriage			

(iv) I prefer love marriage
(v) I prefer arranged marriage
(vi) I prefer to decide jointly with parents
(vii) Sex education in schools in essential
(viii) sex education through textbooks is preferred
(ix) Media like TV, Radio and print media is desirable for learning about sex

9. Abortion
(a) Abortion is legalised Yes/No/Don't know
(b) Is it right to abort when not wanted Yes/No/No opinion
(c) Within what/period (month/plays of conception) abortion is safe without affecting health of the mother?

10. Age at marriage and Child Care and development.
(a) Correct/desirable Age at marriage Boys :
Girls :
(b) After how much gap, it is desirable to have the first child? one yr/2 yr/3 yrs/any other.
(c) Reasons for son preference: Rank the following.
(i) show/receive love
(ii) develop kinship/lineage
(iii) perform last rites
(iv) protect the property
(v) old age support
(vi) help in work/profession
(vii) companionship
(viii) increase income
(ix) get dowry
(x) pride of producing male heir
(xi) any other

11. (i) What should be the birthweight of New born?
(a) 3 Kg (b) 2.5 kg (c) 5 Kg
(ii) How long should Children be breast-fed?
(a) 3 months (b) 6 months (c) 1-2 years
(iii) When do you start supplementary food to children?
(a) after 3 months (b) after 3 months (c) after 1 years
(iv) How often pregnant women should get examined medically?
(a) every months (b) once in thee months (c) after 6 months
(v) How much weight increase should there be for the pregnant women.
(a) 5 Kg (b) 10 Kg (c) 8 Kg (d) Kg

(vi) For what purposes vaccinations/immunizations are done to new borns? What are they?

(viii) Why early marriage is inadvisable?
(a) health will get affected
(b) mental growth will get affected
(c) infants' health will be affected
(d) any other

12. What is raping?

13. What is your opinion on masturbation?

14. Who should determine the birth of the child?
(a) husband (b) wife (c) both
(d) in-laws (e) any other

15. Whose responsibility is child care
(a) Mothers' (b) fathers' (c) joint

16. What child do you desire to have as your first child?
(a) Male (b) Female (c) anything is alright

17. (i) What knowledge/information do you desire to obtain regarding pregnancy and health? Specify.
(ii) What services are required for adolescents in this regard? Specify.
(iii) What counselling services are required in this regard? Specify

18. Knowledge on Aids
(i) Do you know what is AIDS? Yes/No
(ii) Is AIDS curable?
(iii) Give four way of spreading AIDS
(iv) Give four ways for preventing AIDS

19. How do you like to learn about pregnancy, abortions, family planning methods?

Source	To great extent	To some extent	Not at all
(i) Thro, friends & peer group			
(ii) Parents & other elders			
(iii) Medical & Para medical personnel			
(iv) Media			
(v) Any other			

Index